# PIP AND BUNNY: THE CHEEKY OSTRICH

T0002650

The invaluable 'Pip and Bunny' collection is a set of six picture books with an accompanying handbook and e-resources carefully written and illustrated to support the development of visual and literary skills. By inspiring conversation and imagination, the books promote emotional and social literacy in the young reader.

Designed for use within the early years setting or at home, each story explores different areas of social and emotional development. The full set includes:

- six beautifully illustrated picture books with text and vocabulary for each
- a handbook designed to guide the adult in using the books effectively
- 'Talking Points' relating to the child's own world
- 'What's the Word?' picture pages to be photocopied, downloaded or printed for language development
- detailed suggestions as to how to link with other EYFS areas of learning.

The set is designed to be used in both individual and group settings. It will be a valuable resource for teachers, SENCOs (preschool and reception), Early Years Staff (nursery, preschool and reception), EOTAs, Educational Psychologists, Counsellors and Speech Therapists.

**Maureen Glynn** has 25 years' experience teaching primary and secondary age children in mainstream, home school and special school settings, in the UK and Ireland.

First published 2020
by Routledge
2 Park Square, Milton Park, Abingdon, Oxon OX14 4RN

and by Routledge
52 Vanderbilt Avenue, New York, NY 10017

*Routledge is an imprint of the Taylor & Francis Group, an informa business*

© 2020 Maureen Glynn

The right of Maureen Glynn to be identified as author of this work has been asserted by him/her in accordance with sections 77 and 78 of the Copyright, Designs and Patents Act 1988.

All rights reserved. The purchase of this copyright material confers the right on the purchasing institution to photocopy or download pages which bear the eResources icon and a copyright line at the bottom of the page. No other parts of this book may be reprinted or reproduced or utilised in any form or by any electronic, mechanical, or other means, now known or hereafter invented, including photocopying and recording, or in any information storage or retrieval system, without permission in writing from the publishers.

*Trademark notice*: Product or corporate names may be trademarks or registered trademarks, and are used only for identification and explanation without intent to infringe.

*British Library Cataloguing-in-Publication Data*
A catalogue record for this book is available from the British Library

*Library of Congress Cataloging-in-Publication Data*
A catalog record for this book has been requested

ISBN: 978-0-367-19108-5 (pbk)
ISBN: 978-0-429-35497-7 (pbk)

Typeset in Calibri
by Apex CoVantage, LLC

Visit www.Routledge.com/9780367136642

# Book 5 The Cheeky Ostrich

Bunny wakes up and sees
Sammy seagull flying high in the sky.

'Mmm…
I wish I could fly,' sighed Bunny.
'Of course you can,'
squawked Sammy as he swooped
down and
landed on the lawn.

'Hop on my back and we'll go for
a ride.'
Bunny couldn't believe her ears.

This was so exciting!
On she hopped and up they went,
over the house, over the park
and over Pip's school.

'Look!' cried Bunny.
'I can see children in the park!'
'Now I can see Pip's school!'

'Children are running, skipping, climbing and playing hopscotch in the playground.'

'Oh! There's Pip!' shouted Bunny.
'Hello Pip! It's me, Bunny and Sammy, up here!'

But before Pip could look up,
they were gone.
Over the hills and lanes; down
they swooped into the zoo.

Bunny sees lions, tigers,
zebras, leopards and giraffes;
monkeys and elephants too.

'Look at the penguins,' said Sammy.
'They are so funny as they waddle around.'

Bunny spots a lady waving a handkerchief
to tell her friend where she is.

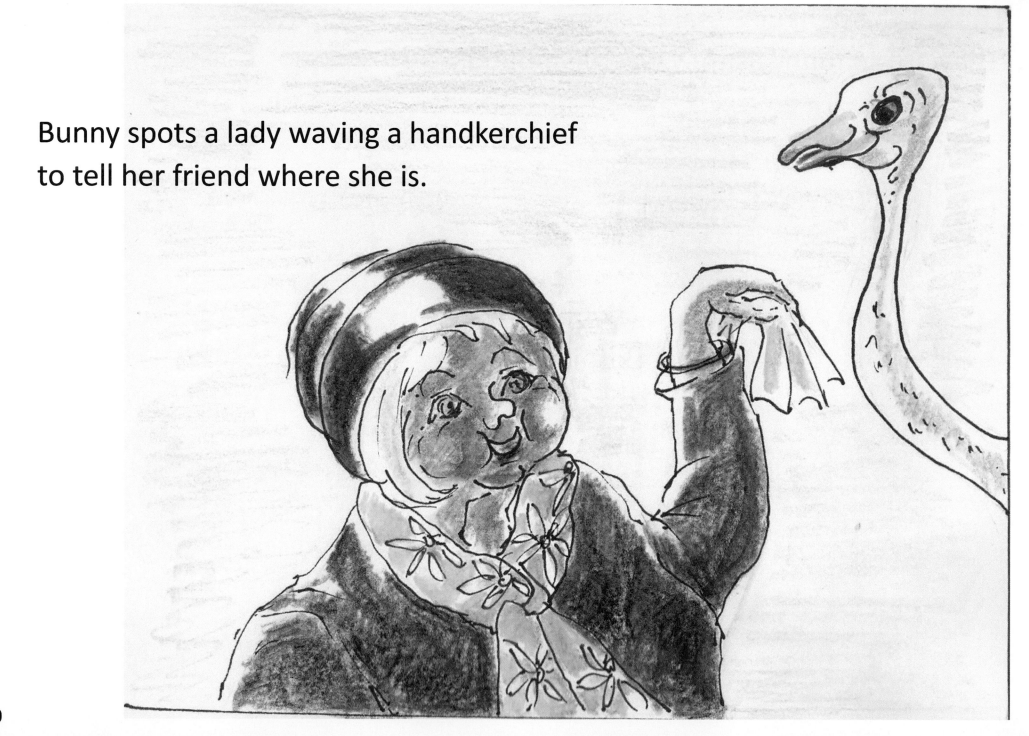

'Oh no!' exclaimed Bunny.
'You won't believe this!'

'That naughty ostrich has snapped up her hanky
and swallowed it whole.'
'Look! There it goes down its neck, bit by bit.'

The lady is surprised and shocked.

The crowd laugh.

'Well I never!' she says. 'What a cheeky ostrich that is!

Fancy eating my hanky, without asking.

No manners! That's what I say.'

Bunny and Sammy laugh too.

'Time to go home now,' said Sammy.
It was great flying today, thought Bunny.

'Thank you Sammy,' she said,
as she slid off the seagull's back,
safely onto the grass at home.

'I can't wait to tell Pip what happened today,' said Bunny.

Pip does enjoy Bunny's story, especially
when she hears about the cheeky ostrich.
She and Bunny laugh together.

Would you laugh too?

**Book 5 The Cheeky Ostrich What's the Word?**

**Show the page and ask the child to say words that explain each image:**

**Page 17 Action Words?**

**Page 18 Location Words?**

**Page 19 Descriptive Words?**

**Page 20 Zoo Words?**

**Page 21 Emotions and Feelings?**

# Action Words?

Copyright material from Maureen Green (2020), *Pip and Bunny: The Cheeky Ostrich*, Routledge

Copyright material from Maureen Green (2020), *Pip and Bunny: The Cheeky Ostrich*, Routledge

# Descriptive Words?

Copyright material from Maureen Green (2020), *Pip and Bunny: The Cheeky Ostrich*, Routledge

Copyright material from Maureen Green (2020), *Pip and Bunny: The Cheeky Ostrich*, Routledge

# Emotions and Feelings?

Copyright material from Maureen Green (2020), *Pip and Bunny: The Cheeky Ostrich*, Routledge